AGEISM

A GLOBAL THREAT

An Easy To Understand Guide On Age Discrimination, Cases, Types, Effects And Actions To End Stereotyping And Prejudice Globally

INTRODUCTION

Ageism is a type of systemic oppression that targets people in a given age range. It primarily affects the elderly, but children and teenagers are also susceptible. It's founded on assumptions like the idea that all older people are unintelligent or disagreeable, or that young people aren't worth listening to.

In the healthcare business, ageism is pervasive, which is especially harmful because as people get older, they are more likely to need medical attention. As a result of this, there is discrimination, poor care, and preventable disease and disability.

CHAPTER ONE

WHAT IS AGEISM EXACTLY?

Ageism or age discrimination occurs when someone treats you unfairly because of your age. It can also refer to how older people are depicted in the media, which has a greater impact on public perceptions.

Ageism has the potential to harm your self-esteem, employment prospects, financial situation, and overall quality of life.

To ensure that no one suffers as a result of their age, ageism must be addressed. You may be perfectly aware that you have been the victim of ageism, but it may not be that clear in some cases.

Although ageism is frequently connected with the workplace, it can also occur while shopping, seeing the doctor, or obtaining goods and services over the phone.

HOW IS AGEISM BEST EXPLAINED?

Age discrimination occurs when persons are treated unfairly because of their age, which is prohibited by international human rights law. The Ontario Human Rights Code prohibits age discrimination in employment, housing, commodities, services, and facilities, contracts, and membership in trade and vocational groups.

In comparison to other forms of prejudice, age discrimination is typically neglected. Nonetheless, it can have the same economic, social, and psychological effects as other forms of prejudice.

To combat ageism, it is critical to raise public knowledge about it and debunk common beliefs and assumptions about aging. Aging is a deeply personal experience, and making broad assumptions about an older person's capabilities and abilities based on their age, just as making broad conclusions about someone based on any other aspect of their identity, is impossible. Human rights principles demand that all people, regardless of age, be treated as individuals and judged on their own merits rather than preconceived notions and that they be given the same opportunities and advantages as everyone else. It is vital to recognize that seniors make significant contributions to society and that we must not limit their potential.

At the same time, ageism can be combated through inclusive planning and design that reflects the conditions of individuals of all ages to the greatest extent possible. The Supreme Court of Canada has ruled that designing systems based on the assumption that everyone is young and then attempting to accommodate persons who do not fit this assumption is no longer appropriate. Instead, to avoid the establishment of physical, mental, and structural barriers, the age variety that exists in society should be represented in the design phases of policies, programs, services, facilities, and so on. Individuals in charge should identify and endeavor to remove any barriers that currently exist.

EXAMPLES OF AGEISM

• getting terminated from a job due to your age

• being denied interest-free credit, a new credit card, auto insurance, or travel insurance because of your age.

• receiving poor service in a business or restaurant as a result of management's attitude toward senior persons

• a doctor refusing to send you to a consultant because you're 'too old'

• being denied membership in a club or trade organization because of your age.

The following are some examples of workplace ageism:

• refusing to hire people who are over or under a certain age limit

• during a job interview, inquiring about someone's age when it has no influence on the work

• establishing rules that favor one age group over another.

• denigrating the elderly as ineffective, useless, or stuck in their ways

• labeling teenagers as inexperienced, irresponsible, or untrustworthy

• Bullying or harassment

Personal relationships can be illustrated by the following examples:

• treating elderly family members as though they were invisible, ignorant, or disposable

• making ageist jokes implying that a person's age makes them less valuable or deserving of respect

• making sexist remarks about a certain generation, such as implying that millennials are entitled

• Disregarding a person's concerns or preferences due to their age

• Taking advantage of someone's age for personal gains, such as making money

• Using a person's age as a means of manipulating, deceiving, or controlling them.

CHAPTER TWO

TYPES OF AGEISM

Ageism can be classified in numerous ways. The terms listed below can be used to define ageism:

1. When an institution's actions and policies foster ageism, this is known as institutional ageism.

2. Age discrimination in social situations (interpersonal ageism).

3. internalized ageism, which occurs when a person internalizes and applies ageist views to himself. Ageism can take many different forms depending on the situation. The assumption that youngsters are violent or dangerous are examples of hostile ageism.

Beneficial ageism, on the other hand, occurs when someone has patronizing attitudes toward people their age, such as thinking of older people as children who require assistance with simple tasks.

It's also necessary to evaluate if the person is conscious of ageism when categorizing it. When they are, they are subjected to open ageism. Implicit ageism happens when people are unaware of their age. Implicit ageism occurs when a clinician unintentionally treats older and younger patients differently.

AGEISM IN THE WORKPLACE

It's terrifying to believe you're being treated unfairly at work. Discrimination in the workplace is a problem that many people face on a daily basis. It shouldn't be this way, but far too many employees fear retaliation from their bosses and can't afford to lose their jobs and benefits.

There are four key signs to look for if you believe you're being discriminated against at work:

Comments with a clear bias in one direction or the other

While your boss or coworkers may be joking, referring to senior employees as "old man" or "grandma" indicates that they are undervalued. Some of the comments are more subtle than others (questions about your retirement plans, for example), but they all aim to mock your age. Keep track of who said what, when they said it, and how they said it.

Employees under the age of 40 are given special consideration.

You might suspect age discrimination based on how younger employees are treated. It's likely that age is a factor in hiring processes if you notice a pattern of older but capable employees being fired in favor of younger employees being hired, or less qualified but younger competitors being promoted. Make a list of who has been promoted and who is far more qualified for each position. Keep note of who is fired based simply on their age and who is hired to replace them. It's possible that replacements will be younger and earn less money.

Favoritism

Another example of younger workers being given preferential treatment. If you see that younger staff have access to the best equipment, are given the best leads, or are given preferential tasks, it's likely that older staff members aren't being treated fairly. Senior staff is most likely being excluded from critical meetings by your manager.

Sudden Downplaying of your Efforts

You've been working yourself to exhaustion since the beginning of your employment with this organization. You've gone above and beyond to attain your objectives and correctly finish your assignments. Your supervisor begins to give you poor performance assessments and punishes you for little errors that you've never had a problem with or that have never been an issue before. If you notice that your boss's or coworkers' attitudes toward you alter when you approach a certain age milestone and you start receiving unpleasant comments for the first time, you may have a valid age discrimination claim.

AGEISM IN HEALTHCARE

Ageism is pervasive in the medical profession around the world. The entire healthcare system, including diagnosis and prognosis, is affected. It has an effect on health-care policies as well as workplace culture.

Patients are handled as though they are children
child talk, which entails speaking to elderly individuals in a childlike manner, utilizing simple vocabulary, expressions of love, or a rhythmic tone of voice, is a common example of benign ageism in healthcare.

Age stereotypes that aren't accurate

In addition, incorrect ideas about aging may lead to inefficient medical therapy. Assuming an elderly patient is less independent than they are, for example, can lead to unnecessary diapering or bed rest. As a result, people become increasingly reliant on others.

Lower levels of health

How people feel about their age, as well as how healthcare providers treat them, can have an impact on their health.

Ageists are much less likely to maintain a healthy lifestyle or develop practices that reduce their chance of getting sick later in life.

Compulsion and violence

Young and old persons may be vulnerable to medical intimidation or violence because they believe their feelings are insignificant. It's possible that employees will be less sympathetic to them, or that they'll be required to follow procedures.

CHAPTER THREE

HOW AGEISM AFFECTS EVERYONE

Ageism has far-reaching ramifications, and it affects more than just individuals. Some of them are as follows:

Increased sickness rates: As people get older, ageism has an impact on their physical and mental health, raising care demands and diminishing quality of life. It's also linked to high-risk habits such as smoking, drinking, and eating a poor diet.

Higher healthcare costs and a lack of health insurance increase poverty. This is particularly difficult for retirees, people who have lost a partner or spouse, and those who are unable to work due to illness or disability. Poverty has a detrimental effect on one's health, creating a vicious cycle.

Ageism has been related to earlier death, leading to a 7.5-year fall in average life expectancy.

HOW TO COMBAT AGEISM

There are three techniques to prevent ageism, according to the World Health Organization:
• increasing awareness of the negative effects of ageism and eliminating myths and biases about the subject
• advances in law and policy that can help to eliminate unfairness and bias
• intergenerational interventions that enhance intergenerational cooperation and empathy

Individuals can aid these efforts by partnering with the Government. Allyship requires investing one's personal time and energy to combatting ageism by doing the following:

- Consider how ageism affects your personal thoughts, feelings, and life experiences while identifying ageism.

- Educate yourself on the topic of ageism to learn more about how ageism affects others, listen to personal stories, read literature, and do research.

- It's critical to learn and practice advocacy skills like knowing when to speak up and when to back off.

- Getting things done: Take what you've learned and put it into practice. Disputing ageist jokes, correcting ageist stereotypes, and speaking out against ageism are all good ideas. It's important to remember that this isn't all about rescuing people; it's solely about supporting and advocating for them in situations where they aren't being heard.

CHAPTER FOUR

HOW THE LAW PROTECTS YOU FROM AGEISM

Discrimination on the basis of age and employment circumstances

Discrimination in the workplace is illegal in all areas, including hiring, firing, remuneration, job assignments, promotions, layoffs, training, benefits, and any other employment term or condition.

Discrimination and Harassment Against Seniors

Harassment based on a person's age is prohibited.

Harassment can take various forms, including making derogatory remarks about someone's age. Simple mocking, offhand comments, or isolated incidents that aren't very serious aren't forbidden, but harassment happens when it is so frequent or severe that it creates a hostile or abuse in the workplace or results in an unfair labor decision (such as the victim being fired or demoted).

The harasser could be the victim's boss, another department's manager, a coworker, or even someone who isn't a firm employee, such as a client or customer.

Discrimination on the basis of age and policies/practices in the workplace

It may be forbidden if a policy or practice that applies to everyone, regardless of age, has a negative impact on applicants or workers aged 40 or older and that is not based on a justifiable factor other than age (RFOA).

CHAPTER FIVE

CONCLUSION

In conclusion, Ageism is a type of injustice that affects everyone because most people grow older, and it must be addressed via education, intergenerational understanding and cooperation, and legislative change.